Breath OF LIFE

LIVING GOD'S PROMISE OF PEACE
in the 7 Dimensions of Wellness

KAREN FERGUSON

Breath of Life by Karen Ferguson, Published by Illuminate Communications LLC, Vancouver, WA 98682
www.illuminatecommunications.org

© 2017 Karen Ferguson
All rights reserved. No portion of this book may be reproduced in any form or by any means without permission from the publisher, except as permitted by U.S. copyright law. For permissions contact:
https://illuminatecommunications.org/contact/

Edited by: Haley Hampton, Cynthia Tucker
Cover and interior designed by: Najdan Mancic
Print ISBN: 978-0-9993611-0-8
eBook ISBN: 978-0-9993611-1-5

This book is intended to encourage and inspire and is not designed to replace the advice of the readers' own fitness, medical, financial, legal, or other qualified professional. Individual readers are solely responsible for their own personal, professional, and healthcare decisions. Be sure to contact your healthcare professional before adopting any new fitness or healthcare practices and in all matters relating to your health, especially if you have existing medical conditions. This work is sold with the understanding that neither the author nor the publisher are held responsible for the results accrued from the advice in this book.

Scripture quotations are taken from The Living Bible copyright ©1971. Used by permission of Tyndale House Publishers, Inc., Carol Stream, Illinois 60188. All rights reserved.

So also is my word. I send it out, and it always produces fruit. It shall accomplish all I want it to and prosper everywhere I send it.

Isaiah 55:11

50 percent of the net proceeds of this book will be donated to charity.

DEDICATION

I dedicate this book to the One who pulled me out of darkness and into His marvelous light. Jesus Christ, my Lord, my Savior, my Friend.

Your words are a flashlight to light the path ahead of me and keep me from stumbling.
Psalm 119:105

ACKNOWLEDGEMENTS

I couldn't close this project without saying a heartfelt thank you to my amazing husband, Rick, and two beautiful daughters, Alyssa and Jennifer. It is your love, encouragement, and support that gives me the courage and optimism to dream big and keep taking steps of faith. I love you!

For free wellness tips, tools, and resources, visit
https://illuminatecommunications.org/contact/

CONTENTS

A PERSONAL WORD FROM THE AUTHOR......7

SPIRITUAL WELLNESS: The Foundation for a Healthy Life.......11

    DAY ONE: *Abiding*......13

    DAY TWO: *Breath Prayers*......17

    DAY THREE: *Called to Worship*......21

PHYSICAL WELLNESS: A Sound Structure......25

    DAY FOUR: *His Temple*......27

    DAY FIVE: *The Bread That Satisfies*......31

    DAY SIX: *Awareness*......35

MENTAL WELLNESS: The Protective Cover......39

    DAY SEVEN: *A Powerful Tool*......41

    DAY EIGHT: *Mind Like Water*......45

    DAY NINE: *Power of Perception*......49

EMOTIONAL WELLNESS: The Heart of Our Home......53

    DAY TEN: *An Optimistic Approach*......55

    DAY ELEVEN: *Father Issues*......59

    DAY TWELVE: *The Acceptance/Approval Wheel*......63

SOCIAL WELLNESS: The Open Door..67

DAY THIRTEEN: *People Priorities*..69

DAY FOURTEEN: *Who Do You Say I Am?*.....................................73

DAY FIFTEEN: *Unconditional Love*..77

VOCATIONAL WELLNESS: The Vehicle That Moves Us..............81

DAY SIXTEEN: *Your Sweet Spot*..83

DAY SEVENTEEN: *Safety Nets*..87

DAY EIGHTEEN: *Serving Joyfully*..91

FINANCIAL WELLNESS: Tools for Security................................95

DAY NINETEEN: *Healthy Boundaries*..97

DAY TWENTY: *Divine Contentment*...101

DAY TWENTY-ONE: *A Cheerful Giver*...105

SALVATION..131

NOTES..133

A PERSONAL WORD FROM THE AUTHOR

Your Journey to Greater Peace and Well-Being

What if I told you that you already have everything you need to live a life of peace, every day? You might roll your eyes and dismiss it as nonsense. Or you might call me crazy. You might even respond with something like, "That's easy for you to say. You don't have to deal with . . .

My spouse.
My kids.
My job.
My bank account."

You'd be right. I don't have to deal with what you are dealing with, and some of you may be dealing with some pretty tough circumstances right now. Perhaps you lost your job, your health, or someone you love. Maybe you are facing a heavy load at work or wondering how you will pay your bills next month. Perhaps it's more than one of these pressures combined that has finally brought you to the boiling point.

Peace, you say? With all I'm going through? That's just crazy.

But it's not. If we believe God's Word (and I'm assuming you do since you picked up this devotional—and if you don't, please read on, as there is something worthwhile in here for you too), then we really can have peace, regardless of what's going on around us. Simply because God promises it.

There was a time in my life when I would have considered that opening statement absurd. After a seven-year battle with a variety of struggles—including two injuries that left me with debilitating pain, my mom's death, family health issues, a job loss, a depleted bank account, and a severed relationship with a mentor whom I adored—I struggled to find even a sliver of peace.

I withdrew and became depressed and anxious. I was overweight and out of shape. I had lost my enthusiasm for life. It was my lowest point as a Christian. Sure, I had struggled before when I was living far from the Lord, but this time was different. I was a *Christian*. And *Christians* are supposed to have it all together, right? I had read about God's promise of peace, so I wondered why I couldn't find it when I needed it most.

At this desperate point I finally stopped looking to outside circumstances for peace, and I went deep with God in search of His presence and His promises. I believed that God's Word was true, as best I could, so I was troubled by the disconnect between what His Word said and how I was living—a disconnect I saw in many people around me.

This led to an intensive discovery process that, by God's grace, transformed me from the inside out. Interestingly, my circumstances didn't change right away—I was still recovering from injuries, was without a job, and we were still selling off possessions to keep up with the bills—but the way I viewed God, myself, and my circumstances had changed. That made all the difference.

I have formatted this twenty-one-day devotional using the seven dimensions of wellness, because I have found that to truly walk in the peace God promises, we must approach our lives holistically and make wise and consistent choices grounded in the Word of God. We are whole beings, after all, meaning every part of our life matters. If we are unhealthy in any one area, we will surely feel it in others. I chose twenty-one days for reading because that is the length of time it usually takes to develop a healthy habit.

Consider this devotional your tool for cultivating healthier habits in each area of your life. Let it challenge you to stay close to God and committed to your wellness. Use it for daily inspiration and practical advice to help you live a healthier, happier, and more peaceful life in the Lord.

One reason most books don't transform us is because we don't stop long enough to take a breath and absorb what we've just read or consider what we could possibly learn from it. To be transformed, we must take time to reflect and meditate. You will find help in this book to do just that. At the end of each devotional is a section called My Daily Breath. Here you will find one or more of the following to aid in your journey:

1. **Contemporary worship song for inspiration**
2. **Scripture verse for meditation**
3. **Question for reflection**
4. **Wellness tip for practical application**

I've heard it said that we can't have a testimony without a test. Although I am still a work in progress, I have learned important lessons from the tests I've endured, and by God's grace I am at a place of greater health and peace because of them—not despite them. My hope is that as you read this devotional, you will benefit from my tests, be touched by my testimony, and forge your own strong testimony as you draw your daily breath from the Lord.

Truly, the Breath of Life is the power of God within us to live in health and peace in every part of our lives. It is the spirit-filled life that begins by breathing in God's truth every day and allowing Him to fill every cell of our being with His goodness. Only then will we enjoy wellness in every dimension.

Blessings as you breathe deep!
Karen

SPIRITUAL WELLNESS

The Foundation for a Healthy Life

"All who listen to my instructions and follow them are wise, like a man who builds his house on a solid rock. Though the rain comes in torrents, and the floods rise and the storm winds beat against his house, it won't collapse, for it is built on rock."
Matthew 7:24–25

DAY ONE

ABIDING

John 15:5

"Yes, I am the Vine; you are the branches. Whoever lives in me and I in him shall produce a large crop of fruit. For apart from me you can't do a thing."

I remember years ago when I landed a job at my church. This was the first time I'd be getting paid to work at a church, and I was thrilled! I was excited to leave the secular workforce with all its petty politics and problems and was sure I'd be spared all that now that I was working in a "spiritual" environment. Boy, was I wrong! The problems were still there and so were the petty politics. People complained. They got grumpy and stressed out. There were cliques and rumors and misunderstandings. It wasn't too long before I was eager to go back into the secular workforce, and I did. Sad but true.

It seems like a cranky Christian should be an oxymoron, doesn't it? The Bible is filled with promises of God's peace, yet research shows that Christians are about as stressed out as those who aren't Christians.[1]

Why is that?

Isaiah 9:6 refers to Jesus as the Prince of Peace:

"For unto us a child is born; unto us a son is given; and the government shall be upon his shoulder. These will be his royal titles: "Wonderful," "Counselor," "The Mighty God," "The Everlasting Father," "The Prince of Peace."

As the ruler of peace, Jesus promised His disciples before He ascended into Heaven,

"I am leaving you with a gift-peace of mind and heart! And the peace I give isn't fragile like the peace the world gives. So don't be troubled or afraid" (John 14:27).

This peace Jesus speaks of is not fickle or transient, like our emotions and circumstances. It's a deep-rooted peace that is not dependent on anything or anyone, other than God. It is a gift from Him that will sustain us in the worst of times and is designed to protect our hearts and minds from fears of any kind.

This is the kind of peace I want, don't you?

So, why do we struggle so often to live in this amazing promise of peace? I think C.S. Lewis did a tremendous job of getting to the heart of the matter when he said,

"God cannot give us a happiness and peace apart from himself because it is not there. There is no such thing." [2]

Galatians 5 lists peace as a fruit of the Spirit. In a practical sense, we know fruit cannot develop apart from the vine. Detached from its source of nourishment, the fruit will wither and die. But isn't this what we often try to do in a spiritual sense? We go to our friends and family when feeling anxious before going to God. We mull over tough decisions and weigh all the reasonable options, rather than get alone with God and ask him what we should do. We fill our lives with distractions instead of taking the time to be still and listen for God's voice.

To overcome the often insurmountable stresses of daily life, we need more than wishful thinking and a strong will; we need the power of God. The secret, then, to living a peaceful, fruitful, God-breathed life is abiding in Jesus. Abiding in Him forms a rock-solid spiritual foundation that will fortify every area of our lives, if we let it. And the practice for building this strong foundation is spending intentional time with Jesus—every day.

I learned the importance of this during a very difficult time in my life. A series of life events had left me battling severe physical and emotional pain. At the time, there was no doubt in my mind that I was a Christian, and I even read the Bible now and then. But somewhere along the way, my passion for God had waned, and I no longer prioritized spending time with Him. Because of this, I lacked the fruit of peace I desperately needed to get through a very tough time, and I struggled—a lot. At that point I got serious about making time alone with God a priority—every day. That simple commitment changed my life.

While it is true that we can talk to God anytime and anywhere, and we should, something transformational happens when we make time alone with Him a priority. It's like fertilizer for our entire being, bringing nourishment to grow the peace of God into every area of our lives. It results in an "unreasonable peace,"[3] as best-selling author Joyce Meyer describes it. Peace that is not dependent upon our circumstances and which can withstand the harsh realities of life.

Wherever you are in relationship with Jesus, remember that He will meet you right there. You don't have to do anything other than come to Him with a sincere heart. This devotional will help you do just that. Use it to get alone with God, either for the first time or once again—even if it's only for twenty minutes a day. That's all the time it will take to get you hooked on spending time with Jesus. You will soon discover how essential this practice is to your well-being and how crucial it is to living God's promise of peace.

MY DAILY BREATH

1. Download your favorite music app and listen to "Abide with Me" by Matt Maher.

2. Read John 15:1–17. Meditate on Jesus's words about the vine and the branches. How is your fruit of peace these days? Use the personal journal pages in the back of this

book to write down an honest assessment (the good, the bad, and the ugly) and commit it to God.

3. Just like time spent with God is essential to our spiritual health, oxygen is essential to our overall health. Unfortunately, most of us don't breathe deep enough throughout the day. Make time at least once a day to find a quiet space and breathe deep for one to two minutes. There are many convenient apps to help you with this (my favorite is Breathe2Relax). Download your favorite one and breathe deep!

DAY TWO

BREATH PRAYERS

James 5:16

The earnest prayer of a righteous man has great power and wonderful results.

There is power in prayer.

Do you believe that? Have you ever tried it? If you're like most people, prayer may be your last resort. Maybe it's because we live in a world that praises independence and self-sufficiency. Maybe it's because we don't really believe God cares enough to listen. Whatever the reason, for most of us, our default is to worry.

When faced with a problem, we ask advice from others, weigh all our options, and perhaps read the latest self-help book. And then we worry. Only when we are overwhelmed do we finally get on our knees before the Lord, literally or figuratively.

Can you relate?

I'm getting better at praying first, but it took a bout with anxiety before I began moving toward the apostle Paul's exhortation to "Always keep praying" (1 Thess. 5:17). The word that threw me in that sentence was "always." I mean, who had the time to "always" pray? I used to think this was impossible, and that it must only apply to first century Christians, who just didn't have that much to do back then. In hindsight, I know my error in thinking had to do with a faulty view of what prayer really is.

For years, I thought prayer was something done in church, with others, or on my knees, but only when the house was quiet. Enter two rambunctious young daughters and our house was hardly ever quiet. So, what's a frazzled mom to do? Ask advice. Weigh the options. Read a book. Worry. What I have uncovered is that God doesn't expect us to wait for the "perfect" time to pray. There is none. He wants to talk with us throughout the day. Every day.

Simply put, prayer is about growing a relationship with God. Just as our earthly relationships with our family and friends will not grow unless we spend time together, sometimes talking and sometimes sitting quietly, so our relationship with God won't grow unless we spend time with Him in the same way.

I think we make prayer too complicated. Have you ever heard children pray? They use simple, honest, and sometimes surprising words straight from the heart. We can learn from them in this respect because prayer is simply talking with God, like you would a friend. It's saying what's on your heart and not what you think you're supposed to say. It's turning off the white noise to listen for His voice.

I've been amazed at how much my life has improved since I started doing this.

One thing that helped to combat my anxious thoughts was to catch them immediately and turn them into short prayers. I stumbled across this practice, called "breath prayers," which has been used by Christians for centuries,[1] and I eagerly adopted it. It quickly became an effective way for me to take troubling thoughts and turn my mind back to the only One who could provide the peace I so desperately needed. It's really a perfect model for what prayer should be: prayer should be as natural to us as breathing.

If you're like me, it's in the hectic moments of life that you forget to pray, and you hold your breath and worry instead. This only leads to stress and can turn into anxiety if left unchecked. Once I started capturing my worries, turning them into breath prayers instead, I noticed a significant decrease in my stress levels. I started worrying less and experiencing God's peace more. My circumstances didn't change right away, but I did.

"And we are sure of this, that he will listen to us whenever we ask him for anything in line with his will" (1 John 5:14).

Our prayers invite and ignite the presence of God in our lives, which is exactly what we need to realize His powerful promise of peace. Fortunately, prayer is not complicated. In fact, God made it so simple that a child can do it.

MY DAILY BREATH

1. Listen to "God Help Me" by Plumb.

2. Meditate and memorize Luke 11:9: *"And so it is with prayer—keep on asking and you will keep on getting; keep on looking and you will keep on finding; knock and the door will be opened."*

3. Is there something you want to bring before the Lord in prayer today? Write out a prayer of faith.

4. Don't allow yourself to entertain negative thoughts, as they will surely drain your energy and your peace. Turn them into breath prayers instead. Here are some examples:

> I give you my worries, Lord.
> I depend on you, Lord.
> Make a way, Lord.
> *And my favorite:*
> Lord, help!

DAY THREE

CALLED TO WORSHIP

John 4:23-24

Jesus replied, "The time is coming, ma'am, when we will no longer be concerned about whether to worship the Father here or in Jerusalem. For it's not where we worship that counts, but how we worship— is our worship spiritual and real? Do we have the Holy Spirit's help? For God is Spirit and we must have his help to worship as we should."

The Merriam-Webster online dictionary defines worship as "extravagant admiration or devotion to an object of esteem." Our culture worships many things: money, fame, power, success, and the people who have these things. For many years, my objects of worship were way off kilter. I was a people pleaser, so I worshiped popularity. I enjoyed shopping, so I worshiped money. I struggled with perfectionism, so I worshiped my accomplishments. And for a long time, I was co-dependent, so I worshiped the unhealthy relationships I thought I couldn't live without. Now don't get me wrong, there is certainly nothing wrong with money, success, or relationships. These are gifts from God. The problem for me was doing the right things for the wrong reasons, and honestly, I felt like a big fake because of it. It was only when God took these things away that I began to understand that He is truly all I need. During the painful, but necessary, pruning process, I discovered I can only live in God's peace when I give Him rightful place as the only One worthy of my worship.

I'm a music lover. Music moves me, and one of my favorite things to do in church is worship God with music. The sermons are great and fellowship is nice, but it's that fifteen minutes of singing that excites and energizes me. But I admit, I can be a bit of a worship snob. I raise and clap my hands and wonder why others don't. I stand and sing out and can't understand why the person next to me sits quietly. Basically, I have a hard time remembering that not everyone is as moved by music as I am. As you can see, I am still a work in progress!

The good news is there is more than one way to worship God.

The Bible says in 1 Samuel 16:7 that God looks at the heart, and genuine worship is all about the heart.

"But the Lord said to Samuel, 'Don't judge by a man's face or height, for this is not the one. I don't make decisions the way you do! Men judge by outward appearance, but I look at a man's thoughts and intentions.'"

We could sing the most beautiful song in church, but if we do it to be noticed (sadly, I've done this), it means nothing. We could give oodles of our money and time, but if we do it to impress others (sadly, I've done this too), it amounts to nothing in God's eyes. You see, the Bible talks about all the amazing things we may do "for Jesus" but which have no value if they are not done in love.

"If I had the gift of being able to speak in other languages without learning them and could speak in every language there is in all of heaven and earth, but didn't love others, I would only be making noise. If I had the gift of prophecy and knew all about what is going to happen in the future, knew everything about everything, but didn't love others, what good would it do? Even if I had the gift of faith so that I could speak to a mountain and make it move, I would still be worth nothing at all without love. If I gave everything I have to poor people, and if I were burned alive for preaching the Gospel but didn't love others, it would be of no value whatever...There are three things that remain—faith, hope, and love—and the greatest of these is love" (1 Cor. 13:1-4, 13).

Without love, our greatest efforts will always fall short, because without God's love as inspiration, we will do the right things for the wrong reasons.

Try as hard as we might, we will not find fulfillment in people, things, or accomplishments. Just ask your favorite celebrity or music artist. They seem to have it all, yet so many of them spiral into selfish and self-destructive habits. Only God can provide genuine satisfaction. And we will only experience His promise of peace when we are devoted to Him, above all else.

For me, it was a hard lesson to learn but so worth it.

MY DAILY BREATH

1. **Listen to "Ever Be" by Aaron Shust.**

2. **Read and meditate on Psalm 100:1–5.**

3. **Being out of balance in any area of our lives destroys our peace and can compromise our health. Is there something or someone that you are holding in high esteem, above the place of God? If so, take a moment to speak out a word of confession and then commit to putting God first in every area of your life.**

PHYSICAL WELLNESS

A Sound Structure

For I can do everything God asks me to with the help of Christ who gives me the strength and power.
Philippians 4:13

DAY FOUR

HIS TEMPLE

Ephesians 6:10

Last of all I want to remind you that your strength must come from the Lord's mighty power within you.

A popular adage in the fitness industry is, "If you don't use it, you lose it." I certainly witnessed this played out painfully clear in my own life.

There was a time when I prided myself for hardly ever taking breaks at work. I thought I was being a good employee because I worked for maximum productivity. After several years stuck at a desk that was not properly set up for my body, I paid for being such a "good" employee. The reward? Near constant pain and an avoidable injury that required more than nine months of physical therapy. It was a wake-up call.

My sedentary, over-stressed lifestyle had finally caught up with me, and my body revolted. I couldn't sit for more than an hour at a time. I woke up in pain, and I went to bed in pain. I had difficulty sleeping, and I became physically, mentally, and emotionally exhausted. I learned the hard way that our body was meant for movement.

Thomas Cureton, well-respected exercise physiologist, also known as the Father of Fitness, explained it like this,

"The human body is the only machine that breaks down when not used. Moreover, it's also the only mechanism that functions better—and more healthily—the more it is put to use." [1]

God did not design our bodies to sit for eight hours a day.

Although you won't find a specific exercise regime in the Bible, God does say that our body is His temple, and we are called to honor Him with it.

"Haven't you yet learned that your body is the home of the Holy Spirit God gave you, and that he lives within you? Your own body does not belong to you. For God has bought you with a great price. So use every part of your body to give glory back to God because he owns it" (1 Cor. 6:19–20).

My pastor, Daniel Fusco, said it well, "We are the vehicle which God uses to spread His love in the world."

It's true that our bodies are temporary, and they won't last forever. But if God says they are His dwelling place here on earth and He wants to use them for His glory, then I would say they are very important. Wouldn't you agree?

Unfortunately, we enjoy so many conveniences these days that it is just too easy for us to remain sedentary, and for some of us, it's a job requirement. This creates a vicious cycle. We feel sluggish because we are out of shape: we are out of shape because we are sedentary. And we don't exercise to get into shape because we feel sluggish from being sedentary.

The only way to stop this mad decline into disease is to get moving, and that requires a choice and commitment on our part. No one else can do this for us. While I suppose God could miraculously work our muscles while we sit and watch our favorite TV show, I can say with certainty He won't. He has given us a free will and a body meant for movement. What we do with our bodies is our decision, and it comes with consequences.

Second to a toxic attitude, I find an unhealthy Christian lifestyle alarming. I suppose I find it so unsettling because I know that the way we care for our bodies is one of the few things we can control (along with our attitude), and it is foundational to living a vibrant, fruitful life. Without a healthy body, it is difficult to find the motivation, energy, and stamina to work with persistence and a sense of purpose.

And it sure is tough to live God's promise of peace when the effects of an unhealthy lifestyle strain us.

Don't get me wrong: I am not proposing that we become obsessed with our bodies. That, too, would be out of balance. But I do believe we should honor God by the way we care for our bodies. When we do, we will feel better and have more energy, and will have much greater peace, regardless of the challenges in our lives.

Let's get moving!

MY DAILY BREATH

1. Listen to "Move" by Toby Mac.

2. **Memorize Acts 17:28,** *"For in him we live and move and are! As one of your own poets says it, 'We are the sons of God.'"*

3. **Just as abiding in Jesus is the foundation for spiritual health, so movement is the foundation for our physical health. Inactivity has become the new smoking in regard to its negative effects on health. Counteract this and adopt a sit for sixty, move for three (minutes) practice. Whether you're working at your desk, watching TV, or driving long distances, make a point to stop once every hour and move. It can be something as simple as standing up, stretching tall, and taking in three deep breaths. Just remember to get up and move!**

DAY FIVE

THE BREAD THAT SATISFIES

Matthew 4:4

"But Jesus told him, 'No! For the Scriptures tell us that bread won't feed men's souls: obedience to every word of God is what we need.'"

Growing up, I had a very high metabolism and a slight frame. I endured my share of jokes about being blown away by the wind, but really, I was happy to eat whatever I wanted, whenever I wanted, without any concern of gaining weight. Even though I was skinny, however, I wasn't necessarily healthy. A shy bookworm by nature, I avoided team sports and spent too much time sitting with my nose in a book. Fast forward several years and add two tough pregnancies, raging hormones, and a lack of self-control, and I had packed on almost seventy pounds.

Enter a popular weight loss program.

It was an expensive but effective system for taking off the pounds. Problem was, I didn't learn how to make sound nutritional choices on my own. Everything was done for me. All I had to do was pop a meal in the microwave and fill in my diet with a few store-bought items. It did the job of taking off the weight, but I was hungry most of the time, and I still didn't feel healthy. I gained most of the weight back within a year.

This led to about five years of yo-yo dieting when I would pack on the pounds, try the newest diet, and lose a few pounds, only to start the cycle all over again. It was a frustrating struggle that shattered my self-esteem. I wasn't happy with my body, and I was disappointed in myself because I didn't have the self-control to make lasting changes.

But when I approached my eating from a spiritual standpoint, I found victory over food.

Jesus is called the Bread of Life, and He is the only One who can truly satisfy.

"Jesus replied, 'I am the Bread of Life. No one coming to me will ever be hungry again. Those believing in me will never thirst'" (John 6:35).

How appropriate that Jesus would link our spiritual satisfaction to our physical appetites. He knows us best. When I struggled with my weight, I would eat for many different reasons that had absolutely nothing to do with my health. I would eat because I was bored, sad, mad, tired, stressed out, or plain dissatisfied with life. When I began to view my eating habits from a spiritual perspective, I realized that so many of my food choices were about trying to fill a void that had nothing to do with an empty stomach. I was starved for meaning and tried to eat my way to a satisfaction I could never attain with food, because it always left me wanting more. Once I started seeking God and praying through my cravings, I began to make better nutritional choices. And once I started making better nutritional choices, I started to feel better: physically and spiritually. I was healthier and happier. Satisfied.

Have you ever been around someone who is hangry? My oldest daughter introduced me to this term, and it's a perfect illustration of what happens when we try to fill a spiritual void with food. Being hangry is a combination of being hungry and angry, and when you see it, you should run in the other direction, as it's not a pretty sight. In a physical sense, it's an imbalance in blood sugar due to a lack of food, or the wrong type of food, and it makes people (and those around them) miserable. All it takes to avoid this, however, is the right food at the right time.

In the same sense, when we try to fill a spiritual void with physical food, it will not sustain us. It's like eating the wrong food at the wrong time, and it creates an imbalance that leaves us malnourished. And sometimes downright angry.

It's hard to walk in God's peace when we are hangry. Filling our lives with sound spiritual nutrition, through God's Word and prayer and praise, as well as making sound dietary choices, will bring the balance we need to live healthy, happy lives that are filled with God's blessing of peace.

MY DAILY BREATH

1. **Listen to "To the Table" by Zach Williams.**

2. **When it comes to eating, the more we chew, the more we are nourished. So it is with meditating on the Word of God: the more we "chew" on it, the more we digest it, and the healthier we become. Chew on this verse today: Isaiah 58:11,** "*And the Lord will guide you continually, and satisfy you with all good things, and keep you healthy, too; and you will be like a well-watered garden, like an ever-flowing spring.*"

3. **There are many popular diets out there. The key is finding one that is balanced and sustainable. Best-selling food author Michael Pollen keeps it simple with the following maxim about healthy eating: "Eat food, not too much, mostly plants."** [1]

*Remember to consult with your doctor before beginning any new diet or nutritional program.

DAY SIX

AWARENESS

Luke 21:34

"Watch out! Don't let my sudden coming catch you unawares; don't let me find you living in careless ease, carousing and drinking, and occupied with the problems of this life, like all the rest of the world."

The first time I met with a psychiatrist was a humbling experience. I had been juggling the roles of wife, mom, and department head for several years and had done so quite successfully. I considered myself smart and capable. I should be able to navigate the stresses of life on my own, I told myself. But a combination of chronic pain, unrealistic demands at work, and a growing struggle with perfectionism threw me headfirst into a bout with depression that I could no longer ignore. Looking back, I realized I had been overlooking the signs of burnout for several months. I hadn't been setting proper boundaries or taking proper care of my body. I had become bitter.

This unhealthy approach to life climaxed with a visit to my doctor's office. As I sat with my doctor and began to explain my aches, pains, and heart palpitations, I burst out crying and was shaking uncontrollably. I knew at this point something had to change.

This began a six-month journey to regain balance in my life, which included meeting weekly with a psychiatrist. Honestly, I struggled with this at first and didn't even tell my husband about it until a few weeks into my appointments. I mean, I was a *Christian*, for goodness sake! I should be able to keep it all together.

In the beginning, I chastised myself for my small faith, but as I continued to meet with the doctor and talk through my anxieties, I realized that this was exactly where I needed to be. Exactly where God wanted me to be, in fact. For so long, I had been stuffing my emotions and hiding my struggles, even from those closest to me. I worried that if I did share, they would think less of me. You see, I had become quite good at keeping up appearances. So good, in fact, that I had forgotten how to be real. With myself and others. God began teaching me to let go of my pride, admit my struggles, and accept the support of others. As I stepped out in obedience, He showed me that He is faithful to cover my imperfections. I walked away from the whole experience stronger and more compassionate with myself and others, and I learned some great coping mechanisms that I still use today to stay balanced. But the most important thing I learned through the struggle was to listen to my Father God.

As I began to deal headfirst with the issues that were feeding my perfectionism and sense of despair, it was as if the scales fell from my eyes. I recognized that I had been moving at an insane pace, carrying things God never meant for me to carry: all in the name of being a capable, confident woman. It was a farce, and it was unsustainable.

Sound familiar?

I think for many women this is far too common, as we try to live up to the unrealistic demands of being all things to all people. The perfect mom, wife, daughter, friend, employee, business owner. You fill in the blank. Whether self-imposed or loaded upon us by outside sources, it's draining and will eventually cause us to crumble if we don't make a change. We may not be able to control the events, people, or circumstances in our lives, but we can control our choices. Will we choose to carry the heavy load ourselves or will we give it to God? Will we try to do it in our own strength or trust that God's strength will empower us?

When we fail to give our burdens to God, we get out of balance, which will eventually take a toll on our health and separate us from God's peace. There is a better way, fortunately, but it will require getting real: with God, with ourselves, and with others.

Are you carrying a heavy load today? I urge you to stop right now and give it to the Father.

MY DAILY BREATH

1. Listen to "O Come to the Altar" by Elevation Worship.

2. Memorize 1 Peter 5:7, *"Let him have all your worries and cares, for he is always thinking about you and watching everything that concerns you."*

3. **Know that it is not God's will that you carry any burden. Try this exercise to release your cares to God:**

    a. **Write out your most pressing concerns on small slips of paper.**
    b. **Commit them into God's capable hands, tearing up and throwing away each one as you cover them with a simple prayer of faith.**
    c. **Ask God for His strength to leave those worries in the garbage where they belong!**

MENTAL WELLNESS

The Protective Cover

We Christians actually do have within us a portion of the very thoughts and mind of Christ.
1 Corinthians 2:16

DAY SEVEN

A POWERFUL TOOL

2 Corinthians 10:5

These weapons can break down every proud argument against God and every wall that can be built to keep men from finding him. With these weapons I can capture rebels and bring them back to God and change them into men whose hearts' desire is obedience to Christ.

Isaiah 26:3 says God will keep in perfect peace him whose mind is steadfast upon Him. What does it mean to be steadfast in the Lord? It means to be in daily, relentless pursuit of His presence, His Word, and His peace. And we won't get there by letting our minds wander and settle on negative, self-defeating thoughts. We must feed our minds on God's breath-infused Word.

I was hit head-on with this truth in 2015. It was a tough year. One I refer to as our "lean year," because we were lean on money, resources, and options. Unavoidable (and some avoidable) circumstances had drained our bank account, causing my husband and I to wonder how we were going to pay the bills. It seemed like one thing after another would tax our already meager resources. Cars broke down. We had to replace the water heater. Medical bills piled up. School expenses were due for our girls. I wondered if we would lose our house or have to file for bankruptcy. It was an unsettling time, but for me personally, this lean time was about more than our finances. Unrelenting what-if scenarios invaded my mind with doubts and fears that I just couldn't shake. Troubling thoughts eroded my confidence and hope, and I got to the point where I felt that I just didn't have anything left to give. I felt ice-cold numb.

Desperate for relief, I started seeking out and saturating my mind with the writings of many godly authors, hoping to find warmth and inspiration from their dark-night experiences. One whom I found especially impactful was Joyce Meyer. If you haven't read her work, you really should. Joyce is a best-selling author and worldwide speaker with an amazing testimony, a firm grasp on the Word of God, and a tenacious commitment to a positive outlook. Through her books and audio recordings, I began to practice standing on the Word of God to take control of my thoughts—so they wouldn't control me. You see, the enemy doesn't have control over us, but he can attack our minds until we become so weary that we give him control. Praise God it doesn't have to be this way!

James 4:7 says, *"So give yourselves humbly to God. Resist the devil and he will flee from you."*

Obtaining this promised victory requires a resolute commitment on our part to feed our minds on good things:

"Fix your thoughts on what is true and good and right. Think about things that are pure and lovely, and dwell on the fine, good things in others. Think about all you can praise God for and be glad about" (Phil. 4:8).

For most of my life, I had been entertaining negative thoughts, without much awareness or concern. Add a year of unusual stress, and the quality of my thoughts had spiraled downward and settled into a dark pit of despair. Fortunately, by God's grace, I was given a sliver of light and strength to get out of that pit, and it came through feeding my mind daily on resources grounded in His truth. As I did that, my hope was restored, my health improved, and I discovered God's restorative peace.

The change may have started in my mind, but it soon

overflowed into every area of my life. As I regained control of my thoughts, my words changed; as my words changed, so did my outlook on life. I came to appreciate just how powerful of a tool the mind really is. It's a gift from God, and we must be diligent to safeguard it, for it is one of the first places the enemy will attack.

Research shows that 75 to 98 percent of mental, physical, and behavioral illness comes from one's thoughts, with negative thinking eroding our body's natural ability to heal itself.[1] Do you desire to live a holistically healthy life? You must address your thought patterns and not let them control you. It is a battle for sure, but one that gets easier with time.

God gives us a free will and a powerful mind to dream, hope, learn, create, and enjoy the world around us. Let's use it to honor Him.

MY DAILY BREATH

1. Listen to "Yes and Amen" by Housefires (Live at Bethel).

2. **Memorize Romans 12:2,** *"Don't copy the behavior and customs of this world, but be a new and different person with a fresh newness in all you do and think. Then you will learn from your own experience how his ways will really satisfy you."*

3. **One mental practice that was illuminating for me was to journal my thoughts for three consecutive days. Boy, was it a revelation! I discovered just how toxic my thinking had become, and I was able to identify unhealthy thinking patterns I had been entertaining for years. The first step toward change is awareness, so give it a try!**

a. Keep a pencil and small journal handy (or use your favorite notes app), and do your best to keep track of all the negative judgments and criticisms that you make throughout the day. This includes those you make about yourself and other seemingly harmless judgments you may make about things like food, TV, new stories, etc. Try to record these as soon as you make them and be as detailed as possible.

b. At the end of the three days, take time to prayerfully read through them, and identify the negative patterns you are struggling with in this season of your life. Bring these to the Lord in prayer and make a commitment to combat them by immediately bringing any negative thought to the Lord every day.

c. Remember to be gracious with yourself. You may be surprised at the initial results of this practice, but rest assured, your thoughts don't define you. This is the first step toward a healthier mind and healthier life!

DAY EIGHT

MIND LIKE WATER

Psalm 107:29–30

He calms the storms and stills the waves. What a blessing is that stillness as he brings them safely into harbor.

I come from a family of worriers. I used to think it was just a part of my DNA. Both my grandmothers were worriers. My mom was too. I have struggled with worry most of my life, and I've seen the struggle in my daughters. I am beginning to understand that, while worry seems to be a common part of the human condition, it does not have to control us.

"Don't worry about anything; instead, pray about everything; tell God your needs, and don't forget to thank him for his answers. If you do this, you will experience God's peace, which is far more wonderful than the human mind can understand. His peace will keep your thoughts and your hearts quiet and at rest as you trust in Christ Jesus" (Phil. 4:6–7).

Sounds simple, doesn't it? Don't worry, just pray. It's like the easy button from Office Depot. Although it may sound like a simple concept, I know from personal experience how hard it can be to live out on a daily basis. But I have discovered one key to realizing this promise: slowing down.

Most of us move at an unreasonable pace these days. Bombarded with an overabundance of information, choices, and tasks on our to-do list, we fail to make regular time to quiet and focus our minds at all, let alone on the Lord. We forget to "be still" and know that He is God as the Bible instructs (Ps. 46:10). No wonder we are stressed-out and burnt-out. We've become accomplished, but superficial, multi-taskers. Rarely affording ourselves the luxury of slowing down long enough to clear the clutter in our minds, which is not only essential for our physical health but for our spiritual health, as well.

This reminds me of a fascinating concept I studied in martial arts, called Miso no Mushin, which can be translated as mind like water. Just as water is flowing and adaptive and can absorb impact before immediately returning to its initial state of stillness, so can the martial artist reach a mental state free from distractions and preconceived notions. One that is open and ready to respond to any circumstance, all with a sense of calm. I found this to be an elusive concept for sure, but one I enjoyed practicing because of the mental clarity and refreshment it gave me.

In a similar sense, God does not call us to a place of inner turmoil but to one of tranquility. He has given us the powerful ability to focus our minds and dismiss the distractions of life, so we can ready them for any circumstance—advancing into even the most difficult of situations armed with the peace that can be found only in Him.

It is simple, really. It only requires that we make time throughout our day to slow down and focus on Him. Only then will we be able to reach this desirable state and enjoy the promise of His incomparable peace.

Breathe deep and be still before God today.

MY DAILY BREATH

1. **Listen to "Still" by Hillary Scott & the Scott Family.**

2. **Read and reflect on Psalm 46.**

3. "The beginning of anxiety is the end of faith; the beginning of true faith is the end of anxiety."[1] What end are you on today—faith or anxiety? Remember, faith and fear (anxiety) cannot co-exist. Renew your commitment to walk by faith today.

4. Here's an exercise to try when you're feeling tense and anxious. It's something you can do just about anytime and anywhere. I have even used it when sitting in stressful committee meetings.

   a. CALM stands for chest, arms, legs, and mouth.

   b. Repeat the word "calm" to yourself as you mentally scan these different areas of your body, recognizing tension, and relaxing your muscles.

   c. Repeat for as long as you need, but aim for at least thirty seconds.

   d. This is a great way to intentionally slow down. Better yet, combine this practice with your breath prayers and focus on the Lord!

DAY NINE

POWER OF PERCEPTION

Colossians 3:2
Let heaven fill your thoughts; don't spend your time worrying about things down here.

"I once was blind, but now I see." It's my favorite line from the classic hymn "Amazing Grace." From a spiritual perspective, it's a welcome reminder of how dramatically my life has been transformed from a very dark and broken place to one of light and love. From a practical standpoint, it's a reminder that our perception defines our reality.

We choose to see.

I read a fascinating true story that drives this point home. In the 1970s, hundreds of refugee women from Cambodia came to live in the United States. These women had endured horrendous suffering and loss in their homeland under the Communist leadership of Pol Pot and the Khmer Rouge army. Millions were killed and injured under that regime, and these women had watched their loved ones brutally tortured and killed—powerless to stop any of it. I can't imagine the hell on earth those women endured.

When they arrived in the United States, it made sense that these women shared a deeply rooted, overwhelming sense of psychological pain. What was interesting was that they also shared a peculiar physical manifestation of that pain. A large percentage of these women could not see. Their vision was impaired, so much so that, for some, they were unable to take care of themselves. What was curious, however, was that in every case, brain imaging tests showed that their visual systems were functioning normally. There was no physical explanation for why they couldn't see. One of the doctors explained it like this, "They just don't want to see anymore."[1]

How about us? How many of us choose not to see?

Whether it's looking past the man or woman on the street in need, ignoring the extra twenty pounds that compromises our health, or focusing on all the negatives in life, too often we *choose* not to see.

Instead, we stumble in the darkness of our own fears and failures—of not being enough, not doing enough, not having enough. We are blinded to our value and worth as individuals created in God's image.

"So God made man like his Maker. Like God did God make man; man and maid did he make them" (Gen. 1:27).

We overlook the extraordinary diversity and beauty that is all around us.

"O Lord, what a variety you have made! And in wisdom you have made them all! The earth is full of your riches. There before me lies the mighty ocean, teeming with life of every kind, both great and small" (Ps. 104:24–25).

Our perceptions are formed in our mind and they are powerful, indeed. They define our reality because they define how we experience this life. It's not necessarily that our circumstances need to change for us to find the peace God promises—it's that we need to change.

We must choose to see.

Sadly, the negative news feed won't go away, and it is easy to grow cynical and afraid. There is pain in this life, and sometimes those closest to us will hurt us. Deeply. But even during the darkest times—when difficulty and pain cloud our vision—there is still remarkable beauty to behold. There is still light and goodness all around us. And there is always hope in Jesus Christ.

We must only choose to see.

MY DAILY BREATH

1. Listen to "Broken Vessels (Amazing Grace)" by Hillsong Worship.

2. Memorize Psalm 18:28: *"You have turned on my light! The Lord my God has made my darkness turn into light."*

3. Are you perceiving something that feels dark and intimidating, causing a heaviness in your spirit? Ask the Lord to illuminate His goodness to you today.

4. Sometimes we just need to slow down long enough to get out of our head and take notice of the beauty and blessings around us. Take time at least once a day (or whenever you feel overwhelmed and overstimulated) to stop:

    a. Take a deep breath into your belly, intentionally letting go of any muscle tension.

    b. Observe your external environment. Focus on your surroundings, and take note of at least three pleasant things, such as colors, shapes, objects, or sounds that you like.

    c. Look for a small detail that you haven't noticed before.

    d. Thank God for His goodness!

EMOTIONAL WELLNESS

The Heart of Our Home

♥

He heals the broken-hearted, binding up their wounds.
Psalm 147:3

DAY TEN

AN OPTIMISTIC APPROACH

Psalm 147:11

But his joy is in those who reverence him, those who expect him to be loving and kind.

"Being positive doesn't mean we deny the existence of difficulty; it means we believe God is greater than our difficulties." — Joyce Meyer

One key to an emotionally healthy life is living with a sense of enthusiasm and optimism. It's this kind of outlook that will help us cope effectively with the difficulties of life, holding onto the hope that no matter what, God is greater and will get us through.

Let's face it, we are all in process. We will never be perfect until we get to heaven. But so often, we choose to focus on what we don't have and what we can't do. When we do this, we invite a host of unstable emotions to flood our mind, which deprives us of the peace that God promises.

God never promised to rid our life of difficulty, and He didn't promise to make us like anyone else either. But He did promise to complete the good work that He began in us.

"And I am sure that God who began the good work within you will keep right on helping you grow in his grace until his task within you is finally finished on that day when Jesus Christ returns" (Phil. 1:6).

Much like a dentist needs our consent before fixing an issue, so we must surrender our consent to God if we want to see the fullness of His good works in our lives.

Surrender does not come easy for many of us. More often, we hold onto strict expectations and agendas with white-knuckled fists, and when things don't go as planned, we get frustrated and angry. We might even pout a bit. And let's face it, things usually don't go as planned, which is why many of us struggle with an overall sense of dissatisfaction with our lives.

I've heard it said that the surest thing to ruin a relationship is expectations. Expectations can also damage our relationship with God. When we hold onto rigid ideas of what we need to be happy, we can become disappointed with God when things don't go exactly as planned. We know in our head that He could give us what we want if He wanted to; I mean after all, He *is* God! So we question in our hearts if He really loves us at all because He did not give us what we want.

It's a vending machine type of faith, really. One where we put something in (prayer) and expect something specific to come out right away. But God is not our big vendor in the sky, and we would be keen to remember that His understanding of our needs and future is so much deeper, higher, and broader than ours, for we are limited in every way. He is not.

"This plan of mine is not what you would work out, neither are my thoughts the same as yours! For just as the heavens are higher than the earth, so are my ways higher than yours, and my thoughts than yours" (Isa. 55:8–9).

Fortunately, God has not left us in the dark when it comes to His plans and His ways. He has given us His spirit-breathed Word of Life, the Bible, and if we seek Him diligently through it, we will grow in our understanding of His thoughts and His ways and can better align our desires with His.

I heard an analogy once about the difference between expectations and expectancy. Basically, the difference is what holds them. Expectations are bound in a rigid box filled with limitations of certain things, done a certain way, and at a certain time for us to find satisfaction. Expectancy, however, is a sense of hope carried loosely with open hands and an open heart.[1]

What are you holding onto today? A set of fixed plans for your life or a confident sense that God will do something good in your life? Our emotions and desires can be fickle and will sometimes change by the moment, it seems. But fortunately, God never changes.

"Jesus Christ is the same yesterday, today, and forever" (Heb. 13:8).

When we come to God with hope, surrendering our emotions and plans with open hands, God's peace will sustain us, even when things don't go as planned. Embrace a sense of optimism for your future today, knowing that God is higher, He is able, and He is good. God has great things in store for you!

MY DAILY BREATH

1. **Listen to "Trust in You" by Lauren Daigle.**

2. **God's Word says that He has a good plan for your life. Memorize and meditate on Jeremiah 29:11,** *"For I know the plans I have for you, says the Lord. They are plans for good and not for evil, to give you a future and a hope."*

3. **What are you hoping for today? Write out a list and surrender these things to the Lord in prayer.**

DAY ELEVEN

FATHER ISSUES

Psalm 68:5–6

He is a father to the fatherless; He gives justice to the widows, for He is holy. He gives families to the lonely and releases prisoners from jail, singing with joy.

I read an interesting, but sad, statistic. According to the U.S. Census Bureau, one in three children live without their biological father in the home. Some call this a "father absence crisis," as there is an absent father in nearly all of America's ills, including poverty, teen pregnancy, crime, incarceration, and drug abuse.[1] Unfortunately, the number of single-parent households only continues to grow.

One could argue that there is a Father absence crisis in the Church, as well, as I've talked to many people who have a hard time connecting to the Father God. It's not that the Father is absent but that we fail to connect with Him.

The Bible says that God is a triune being: Father, Son, and Holy Spirit. Three distinct, but co-equal and co-eternal, persons in the Godhead. I think for many it can be easier to connect with Jesus, because the New Testament is filled with stories of His goodness, love, and compassion toward people like us. The Bible says He was a friend to sinners and the common people heard him gladly. He slept, ate, laughed, cried, worked, and sometimes got angry. This makes him relatable. But the Father? Not so much.

We can easily get stuck in an Old Testament mindset where we view the Father as a holy but harsh God with unrealistic expectations who is eager to dole out severe punishment. And sometimes we might approach him from a purely emotional perspective based on our past experiences with people who have hurt us, even our own imperfect earthly fathers. But Jesus said that when we see Him, we see the Father.

"Jesus replied, 'Don't you even yet know who I am, Philip, even after all this time I have been with you? Anyone who has seen me has seen the Father! So why are you asking to see him?'" (John 14:9).

In fact, He said that He could only do what He sees His Father doing.

"Jesus replied, 'The Son can do nothing by himself. He does only what he sees the Father doing, and in the same way'" (John 5:19).

This means when we see Jesus's love, patience, grace, and selfless sacrifice poured out on the pages of the Bible, we see the heart of the Father.

A perfect illustration of the Father's love is found in Luke 15:11–32. Here was a selfish son who abandoned his father, took his property, and spent it on wild parties and prostitutes in a distant country. Only after much pain and poverty did the son decide to go back to his father and ask for forgiveness. He was out of money and out of options, so he was willing to bear the punishment of his father and expected only to work for him as a servant.

One verse paints such a beautiful picture of the Father God's love for us, and it's my absolute favorite. It says,

"So he returned to his father. And while he was still a long distance away, his father saw him coming, and he was filled with loving pity and ran and embraced him and kissed him" (Luke 15:20).

Soak that in for a moment. The father had been watching and waiting for his son to come home. He was looking for him. And when he did return, the father didn't chastise him and heap him with a load of guilt. He ran and embraced him. He even threw a celebration party! Now, *that* is unconditional love. And that is the sort of love the Father has for you and me. He doesn't condemn or reject us; He pursues us and calls us His own. He has invited you and me to be a part of His forever family, and He gave His Only Son, Jesus, to make that happen.

If we want to enjoy greater emotional well-being, we must engage in satisfying relationships based on trust and respect. This includes our relationship with the Father God.

I can say with confidence that when we seek to understand and accept the Father's unconditional love, we will enjoy greater emotional stability and truly find His peace in the storms of this life.

Draw near to Father God today.

MY DAILY BREATH

1. Listen to "Good, Good Father" by Chris Tomlin.

2. Meditate on these verses: Romans 8:15–16, *"And so we should not be like cringing, fearful slaves, but we should behave like God's very own children, adopted into the bosom of his family, and calling to him, 'Father, Father.' For his Holy Spirit speaks to us deep in our hearts and tells us that we really are God's children."*

3. John 14 refers to God as our Father more than twenty times. Read this text aloud and consider if your view of God the Father needs to change.

4. Part of being an emotionally healthy person is the ability to forgive those who have offended or hurt us. Who do you need to forgive today? Write out a prayer of forgiveness.

DAY TWELVE

THE ACCEPTANCE/APPROVAL WHEEL

Romans 15:7

So warmly welcome each other into the church, just as Christ has warmly welcomed you, then God will be glorified.

Growing up, I was quite the people pleaser. I was afraid of offending people, afraid of disappointing people, and afraid of not fitting in. Perhaps it was because I suffered a lot of rejection and ridicule in my early years. Or maybe it had to do with my birth order or personality type. Whatever the reasons, my desire to be accepted at all costs caused me to make many foolish and sometimes self-destructive decisions. I had become so adept at playing chameleon, changing my traits and behaviors on a whim to suit others, that I got to the point where I didn't even know my true self. And I questioned if my truest self would ever be good enough.

At one point, I suffered a kind of identity crisis that caused me to retreat and isolate myself from others for a period of time. It also gave me an opportunity to step off the self-defeating approval/acceptance wheel so I could discover my true identity. In Christ.

I think most of us can relate to the desire to be accepted by others. At some level, we all want to be a part of the "in" crowd. We like the approval of others. It makes us feel important, like we matter. The problem is trying to please others keeps us from living an authentic life. It can also keep us from serving God, because the desire to please people can make us timid in our faith.

The Bible says the Word of God is living and powerful.

"For whatever God says to us is full of living power; it is sharper than the sharpest dagger, cutting swift and deep into our innermost thoughts and desires with all their parts, exposing us for what we really are" (Heb. 4:12).

The Word of God can also be offensive to those who don't believe. Jesus said on many occasions that we should expect suffering and persecution for no other reason than because we follow Him.

1 John 3:13 says, *"So don't be surprised, dear friends, if the world hates you."*

John 15:18 tell us, *"For you get enough hate from the world! But then, it hated me before it hated you."*

This can be hard to swallow for a people pleaser!

I don't know of anyone who is eager to be hated or persecuted, but for those of us who place our identity in the acceptance of others, statements like those make us want to play like a turtle and retreat into our shell. We don't want to be "hated" by others, so we look the other way and keep quiet. We don't share our testimony with our neighbor or invite that co-worker to church for fear of rejection. We stand silent in our community because we don't want to be labeled a religious freak.

Can you relate at all?

"And then he told them, 'You are to go into all the world and preach the Good News to everyone, everywhere'" (Mark 16:15).

There is a dying world that needs to hear the good news of eternal life in Jesus, and God has not called you and me to be silent. He has called us to be His bold witnesses. To be salt and light to a tasteless and dark world.

To find the power to fulfill this purpose of God in our lives, we must jump off the acceptance/approval wheel and resolve to please only One person—God, who made us and wants to use us for His divine purposes.

The best remedy I have found for a people pleaser? Discover your unique identity in Christ. Embrace the truth that you are created in the image of God (Gen. 1:27) and loved completely. Believe that God has a good plan for your life, and that He is faithful to complete the good work He began in you.

Fortunately, we don't have to change anything about ourselves to be accepted by God. He already accepts us just as we are. But to live an emotionally healthy life powered by God's peace, we must keep our priorities in check. And that will require a bold change on our part.

Are we living to please others or God? Are we trying to fit in with the world or are we okay with being different? To hide our beliefs and live an inauthentic life will damage our identity and drain the peace of God right out of our lives. Only when we step off the acceptance/approval wheel can we truly discover who God created us to be and become the bold witnesses He has called us to be.

MY DAILY BREATH

1. Listen to "In Christ Alone" by Kristian Stanfill.

2. Read Psalm 139. Always remember, you are fearfully and wonderfully made by the God who created the universe. Amazing!

3. Write out a list of your unique qualities, quirky ones and all. Say a breath prayer of thanks to the Lord throughout this week for the way He made you. Whenever you start to doubt your worth, think of at least three of these things that you like about yourself (or could learn to like).

SOCIAL WELLNESS

The Open Door

Let the peace of heart that comes from Christ be always present in your hearts and lives, for this is your responsibility and privilege as members of his body. And always be thankful.
Colossians 3:15

DAY THIRTEEN

PEOPLE PRIORITIES

Hebrews 10:24–25

In response to all he has done for us, let us outdo each other in being helpful and kind to each other and in doing good. Let us not neglect our church meetings, as some people do, but encourage and warn each other, especially now that the day of his coming back again is drawing near.

Have you ever heard someone say, "I don't have to go to church to be a Christian"? I have. Perhaps you've said it yourself. While it's true, what is also true is that God designed us for community.

"But if we are living in the light of God's presence, just as Christ does, then we have wonderful fellowship and joy with each other, and the blood of Jesus his Son cleanses us from every sin" (1 John 1:7).

God created us to connect with each other and remain in fellowship. For our benefit, yes, but also to show the world that we belong to Him.

"Your strong love for each other will prove to the world that you are my disciples" (John 13:35).

If we want to live healthy, balanced lives that align with God's Word, then maintaining social connections is essential. My oldest daughter has taught me a lot in this respect. I'm learning to keep my priorities straight by watching how she makes people a priority in her life.

You see, I'm an introvert by nature. I've never needed much outside stimulation to be content. Just give me a book, a little sunshine, and a comfortable environment, and I'm happy. I adore my family, without a doubt, and I am blessed to have a few close friends, but really, I'm fine being by myself a lot of the time. I suppose that's why writing is such a great fit for me. I don't mind spending long periods of time on my own, ruminating ideas in my head.

Now, before I paint a portrait of myself as a socially awkward, anti-social person, I must point out that I do quite well in most social situations. I'm usually one of the first to smile and engage others in conversation, but I do find that after a few hours in a group setting, I need time to myself to recharge. It's just part of my nature.

Unfortunately, a common myth exists in our society that something is wrong with introverts, which couldn't be further from the truth! Introversion is a personality trait, not a disorder. Introverts are known to be thoughtful contributors to our society. They are creative and cooperative and make up anywhere from one third to one half of our population, depending on which source you read (and how many introverts may have been pretending to be extroverts).[1] So, if you are an introvert, no shame! Seize your own unique strengths and proudly take your place among the likes of Isaac Newton, Albert Einstein, Rosa Parks, and Dr. Seuss, to name a few. And if you aren't one, please remember that God is the creator of diversity and that we introverts have many wonderful qualities to offer society.

But back to people priorities. I'm getting better about not using my introversion as an excuse to avoid making meaningful connections with others. I may be an introvert, but I am called to follow Jesus's example as portrayed in the Bible, and He was all about people. He noticed them. He talked with them. He taught them, He ate with them, and He touched them. It may not come as easy for me as it does for my daughter, but I am inspired to slow down and make more time for others by watching the way she values the people in her life by wholeheartedly reaching out, encouraging, and including others.

Thanks to her example, I am getting better at willingly and cheerfully setting aside my to-do list to check in and do life with the people God has placed in my life.

Ironically, I find that when I do, I am stronger in my faith and more at peace.

"And one standing alone can be attacked and defeated, but two can stand back-to-back and conquer; three is even better, for a triple braided cord is not easily broken" (Eccles. 4:12).

There is strength in numbers. As one who tends to pride myself on being independent, I must resist the urge to "do it" all on my own, and instead make a point to build a network of people I trust and can go to for advice and support. This type of interdependent lifestyle promotes greater well-being, greater productivity, greater results, and greater security. In fact, people who form strong social connections are known to have lower levels of anxiety and depression, stronger immune systems, higher self-esteems, and may recover from disease faster.[2]

Human connection is not only good for our health, it is part of God's divine plan for us. And when we walk in obedience to His plan, we will always enjoy greater peace.

MY DAILY BREATH

1. Listen to "If We Are the Body" by Casting Crowns.

2. **Memorize Romans 12:10**, *"Love each other with brotherly affection and take delight in honoring each other."*

3. My pastor says that there are only three things in life that will last: God, God's Word, and people. How can you make these three more of a priority in your life? Be specific and write it down.

DAY FOURTEEN

WHO DO YOU SAY I AM?

1 Peter 3:15

Quietly trust yourself to Christ your Lord, and if anybody asks why you believe as you do, be ready to tell him, and do it in a gentle and respectful way.

Jesus had been with His disciples in the community. People were drawn to Him, intrigued by Him, and talking about Him. But these were the men who knew Him best. These twelve had been with Him from the beginning of His ministry. They ate with Him, traveled with Him, learned from Him, and just hung out with Him.

After Jesus asked them what the people were saying about Him, He directed His next question to them personally, asking *"Who do you think I am?"* (Matt. 16:15).

Peter enthusiastically answers, *"The Christ, the Messiah, the Son of the living God"* (Matt. 16:16).

Don't you just love it when you answer the teacher's question correctly? Because of Peter's bold response, he has now advanced onto the Good Teacher's A++ list.

"Blessed are you, Simon, son of Jonah," Jesus said, *"for my Father in heaven has personally revealed this to you—this is not from any human source"* (Matt. 16:17).

By God's grace, Peter got it. He was given spiritual understanding of who Jesus really was. Something that many in their community had not yet encountered.

But isn't Jesus's question a little peculiar? Throughout the gospels Jesus doesn't appear to be concerned about people's opinions. He doesn't compete for attention or carefully design His responses to please the majority. So why is He so interested in what people think at this point in His ministry?

I don't think the question was for His own benefit at all, but for the benefit of His disciples. Jesus knew these men had been called to represent Him on earth and that once He returned to heaven, they would be the ones to build His Church. These men were called to change the world, and they did so by His grace and in His strength. But before they could share the gospel truth with others, they needed to come to an internal understanding of who Jesus really was. I think this question is important for each of us to answer.

Who is Jesus?

Some call Him a great teacher. Others a good man. And some call Him a prophet. But who do you say He is? Coming to terms with your own answer is imperative because the world is watching and listening.

Unfortunately, our culture often depicts Jesus in an inaccurate light that leaves spiritually hungry populations without hope. Many try to lump Him in with other teachers and prophets, like Muhammad, Buddha, or Confucius, but what sets Jesus apart from the rest is you won't find Him in His tomb. He is risen!

Visit the memorial sites of these other men, and you will be able to pay respects because they were buried there, and their bones or ashes remain. Not Jesus. He is very much alive and working within His Church.

Too many people selectively choose what they want to believe in the Bible. They acknowledge that Jesus was kind and loving and generous and that He said many good things, but they fail to get the main point of it all. That He is the One and Only true and living God, and the only One who can fill up our deepest longings, granting us eternal hope and abundant life. Here on earth and into eternity. This fact separates Jesus from all other teachers, leaders, and prophets.

C.S. Lewis made a great point about this idea of lumping Jesus in with other religious leaders, when he argued,

"Either this man was, and is, the Son of God, or else a madman or something worse."[1]

If someone claimed they were God and the only way to heaven, would you really take seriously anything else they said? No.

Unless it were true.

Jesus made it clear,

"I am the Way—yes, and the Truth and the Life. No one can get to the Father except by means of me" (John 14:6).

Time is short. You and I are called to represent Christ on earth. We are called to give an account of our faith. Are we ready?

Who do you say Jesus is?

MY DAILY BREATH

1. Listen to "Breathe on Us" By Kari Jobe.

2. Memorize John 14:26, *"But when the Father sends the Comforter instead of me— and by the Comforter I mean the Holy Spirit— he will teach you much, as well as remind you of everything I myself have told you."*

3. You were given God's Spirit when you accepted Jesus as your Lord and Savior. And His role is to teach you and empower you to share the good news of Jesus Christ. The question is, does the Spirit have all of you?

4. Write out a list of people who you know need to hear the good news and ask God to provide you with the courage, strength, and opportunity to share with them. Watch for opportunities, they will come!

DAY FIFTEEN

UNCONDITIONAL LOVE

John 15:9

"I have loved you even as the Father has loved me. Live within my love."

For most of my life, I struggled to feel worthy of love. A history of rejection and abuse left me feeling unlovely, unworthy, and broken. I doubted I would ever find a man who would treat me with respect, let alone love me enough to marry me and start a family. But God has a way of surprising us with the miraculous when we least expect it. And this is what He did for me and my husband.

One chance meeting, divinely orchestrated twenty-six years ago, led to a fairy tale wedding, two beautiful daughters, and twenty-five years spent doing life with my best friend. Although our marriage has not been perfect (no marriage is), I have learned so much about the love of God through my husband. My husband's generous display of love, patience, support, and affection has helped me to open my heart more to others and, most importantly, to God.

I understand that the idea of unconditional love might be a bit hard to swallow for some. Like when you take a shot of vinegar, you might pucker in disbelief. Maybe you've suffered a recent divorce or are in an unhealthy relationship. Perhaps you just haven't met the right man yet or have never been pursued by a man at all.

The longing for a deep, romantic love in which we are cherished and accepted runs deep for most women, and finding that may seem like an impossibility to you. I know it did for me. Human love is flawed and often dependent upon what we do, not who we are, so it can be hard to hope for more. People hurt us, and it can be difficult to warm up once we have been burned. But regardless of your relationship status, the point I'd like to make here is this: relationships are meant to be blessings in our lives, and the good ones are gifts from God; however, we are not called to put our hope or trust in the love of anyone other than God.

As wonderful as my husband is (and he really is!), I have learned to keep our relationship in its proper place. Anytime I looked to Rick for my self-worth and satisfaction instead of to God, my life has gotten out of balance and I've been horribly disappointed. Not because Rick is a terrible person or because he necessarily did something terrible, but because he was never designed to take the place of God in my life.

God is the only One who can love you and me unconditionally—all the time. And He is the only One who can give us the perfect peace we long for. Attempting to find our worth and peace anyplace else, or in anyone else, is a mistake that will only lead to disappointment and pain.

If you have any doubts today that you are loved, take time to remember the sacrifice Jesus made for you. He came to earth to live within the confines of a human body. For you. He endured rejection, ridicule, and eventually a violent death. For you. He rose again, claiming victory over death and sin for you and for me. And for anyone who would call upon Him. He did all this because He loves us that much!

People will let you down, yes, but the Bible says that nothing can separate you from God's love. If you are feeling unloved today, choose to rest in the truth that the same God who created the universe breathed His life into you. You are not a mistake; God made you on purpose and He loves you just as you are. He knows everything about you and chooses to call you His own. Just the way you are. And He will never leave you. Ever.

"For I am convinced that nothing can ever separate us from his love. Death can't, and life can't. The angels won't, and all the powers of hell itself cannot keep God's love away. Our fears for today, our worries about tomorrow, or where we are —high above the sky, or in the deepest ocean — nothing will ever be able to separate us from the love of God demonstrated by our Lord Jesus Christ when he died for us" (Rom. 8:38–39).

MY DAILY BREATH

1. Listen to "Mine" by Hollyn.

2. There is no limit to God's love for you. Read and meditate on Ephesians 3:17–19.

3. Do you believe that God loves you, perfectly and unconditionally, just as you are right now? If you hesitate in answering this question, spend some time journaling why that is.

VOCATIONAL WELLNESS

The Vehicle That Moves Us

Not by might, nor by power, but by my Spirit, says the Lord Almighty—you will succeed because of my Spirit.
Zechariah 4:6

DAY SIXTEEN

YOUR SWEET SPOT

1 Corinthians 12:7

The Holy Spirit displays God's power through each of us as a means of helping the entire church.

You may have heard the phrase, "Choose a job you love, and you will never have to work a day in your life."[1] Unfortunately, statistics show that most of us do not love what we do. In fact, a recent Gallup survey found that 70 percent of Americans are not happy at their jobs.[2] This is significant considering that most people spend the majority of their day working, relative to doing other things.

Being miserable at something that takes up so much time and energy will eventually take its toll, and filling a role that doesn't suit us will lead to chronic stress, which can eventually lead to a host of other largely avoidable diseases. This is why it is important to find your sweet spot, the place where your interests, strengths, and values align. Where work just doesn't feel that much like work. That satisfying place where we forfeit the strain for a sense of fulfillment and ultimately experience greater peace because we are working from a place of strength, not struggle. Sound too good to be true? That's what I thought too. But after much reading and reflection, I am convinced that everyone has a sweet spot. We only have to do some work to find it.

As a forty-something wife and mother, I have only begun to

discover this place. You see, I grew up in a practical household. Although I was taught to have a strong work ethic, I wasn't encouraged to dream big or even advised to discover what I was good at or what I enjoyed doing. Instead, I was told to *"choose wisely."* This meant taking the safe route. Find honest work for a fair wage, no matter how boring or meaningless it might be. If I could do it over again, I'd dream bigger, take more risks, and make the time to do the deep work necessary to find my unique sweet spot. Fortunately, I have discovered that with God it's never too late to move into our passions and purposes.

The Bible has a lot to say about work, and contrary to what some believe, it isn't all bad! The Bible mentions work over 800 times, and it basically says that work is good, God ordains it, and we are to honor him with it.

I've heard some argue that work is a result of the curse (perhaps to justify how miserable they are in their jobs), but that just isn't true. God was the originator of work when He created the world and all that's in it in just six days. He provided a model for work-life balance with six days of work and one day of rest each week. And He gave Adam worthwhile work to do in the garden, even before the fall. Still not convinced? Read the Book of Proverbs, and you'll see numerous references to the value of work, along with best practices for doing it in a way that honors God and blesses others.

I believe that too many of us have been robbed of the blessings God intends to give us through our work because we have settled for positions that don't fit us. I know firsthand how hard it can be to work with peace and passion when you just don't like what you do. I am also a realist and understand that most of us just can't up and leave our positions, no matter how poor a fit they are. We have bills to pay and families to take care of. People are counting on us. I've been there. In fact, I had become so comfortable with the benefits and pay of my last position that I put off looking for a better fit for upwards of two years. I was scared to step out and try something new because, if I did,

I knew I'd have to give up something, whether that was a healthy salary, vacation hours, or a paid parking space. Not until my performance began to slide and my peace was severely shaken did I consult with God and commit to do the internal work of identifying my interests, strengths, and values. I prayerfully took intentional steps to move on. Now, I'm no longer stuck. I'm touching closer to my sweet spot every day, and I'm finding it truly is a position of peace.

Have you ever stopped to think about what you are passionate about? What moves you, excites you, and energizes you? If you can tap into this, and link it to your work, then you really won't need to work a day in your life. You'll be so fueled by your passion that it will fill you with the sustained energy needed to overcome any challenges you face along the way.

Regardless of what you do or where you do it, know that your work matters to God. He has created you with an individuality that is all your own, and He desires to use you for His glory if you let Him. But it will require faith and persistence. It will require doing the internal work of discovering God's calling, which can be a time-consuming and sometimes messy process. But it's rich with possibility, as it is in that place where you will operate with the greatest ease, the least resistance, and the greatest power. It is that place where you can use your work to worship God and be a blessing to others.

MY DAILY BREATH

1. **Listen to "Revelation" by Third Day.**

2. **Consider 1 Peter 4:11,** *"Are you called to preach? Then preach as though God himself were speaking through you. Are you called to help others? Do it with all the strength and energy that God supplies so that God will be glorified through Jesus Christ—to him be glory and power forever and ever. Amen."*

3. There are tons of career development books out there, and I encourage you to get one and work through the exercises. You will gain clarity about yourself: your strengths, interests, and optimal conditions for your most productive work. But if you are looking to discover your calling and not just a career, then I urge you to get quiet before the Lord and ask Him for revelation. He knows you best, and He has already designed you for good works (Eph. 2:10). Ask Him to begin to reveal your sweet spot.

4. No matter where you are in the journey to your sweet spot, whether you've arrived or are stuck in a place that you honestly can't stand, think about what this means for your present position and condition: *"Work becomes worship when you dedicate it to God and perform it with an awareness of his presence."*[8]

DAY SEVENTEEN

SAFETY NETS

Hebrews 11:6

You can never please God without faith, without depending on Him. Anyone who wants to come to God must believe that there is a God and that He rewards those who sincerely look for Him.

Nik Wallenda is either the craziest person you will ever meet or the bravest. On June 22, 2013, he walked across the Grand Canyon on a tightrope suspended 1,500 feet in the air—without a safety net. I remember watching it live on television, eyes glued to the screen, with tight fists and clenched jaw, willing him in my mind to survive this record-breaking feat. He survived, thankfully, and I could breathe again.

Nik has a fascinating history. He comes from seven generations of high-risk, high-wire aerialists and has been walking on wires since he was two years old. He's earned seven Guinness World Records and even re-created the very stunt that had taken his great-grandfather's life. The guy is fearless. He's also a believer, saturating his amazing stunts with prayer and praise. Crazy or not, the guy has incredible courage. He's a risk-taker who took his grandfather's advice to heart when he said that safety nets give a false sense of security.[1] Nik doesn't trust in them. Which made me think—how many of us go through life setting up our own safety nets that are intended to shield us from harm but only keep us from realizing our dreams and living up to our greatest potential?

"The will of God is not safe." –Mark Batterson

I interpret this to mean that God's will for us is usually just outside of our comfort zone and will often require a bold step of faith to get there.

Matthew 17:20 says, *"Jesus told them, 'For if you had faith even as small as a tiny mustard seed, you could say to this mountain, "Move!" and it would go far away. Nothing would be impossible.'"*

If you are anything like me, you may have a hard time believing this audacious statement and have instead set up your own false safety nets, whether it's your savings account, salary, credentials, or experience. Maybe you haven't taken that leap of faith yet because you don't feel prepared enough or "qualified" enough. Too often, we fear failure, so we make every excuse in the world as to why we don't even try. We are waiting for the right safety nets to be put in place first, just in case we fall.

I speak from personal experience. As a small-business owner, it took me too long to get up the courage to step out and get started. Owning a business had been on my heart for several years, but I I had let doubts get in the way of stepping into what I believed God wanted me to do. I ignored the promptings of the Holy Spirit for so long that I had become paralyzed with fear to the point where I doubted if I had ever heard from God at all. In hindsight, I realize that I had become burdened with a sense of hopelessness because I was out of God's will. I wasn't pursuing the dream that He had birthed within me because I was placing my trust in false safety nets rather than in the only One who could keep me safe.

In the beginning, I used the excuse that I was trying to be wise by not making rash, foolish decisions. But when the weight of my hopelessness drained my health, I got real with the Lord and repented of my disobedience. I started walking by faith.

I can't say that I've taken Grand Canyon-style steps of faith up until this point, but I have been consistent about taking small ones, and by God's grace, I'm seeing progress. It's not easy, and the fears and doubts still rear their ugly heads at times, but I can say I am happier and more fulfilled than I have been in years, because I am following what I believe God has called me to do. I have rediscovered the pleasure of God's peace.

Finding our passions and purpose will require us to remove our false safety nets and prayerfully take daily steps of faith in obedience to God. When we do this, we will experience the peace God promises us, despite the challenges. And rest assured, the Father will be right there with us all along the way.

What safety nets do you need to get rid of?

MY DAILY BREATH

1. Listen to "Oceans" by Hillsong United.

2. Memorize Proverbs 13:12, *"Hope deferred makes the heart sick; but when dreams come true at last, there is life and joy."*

3. What hidden dreams do you have? Nik Wallenda said, "I've trained all my life to not be distracted by distractions."[2] What is distracting you from fulfilling your dreams?

DAY EIGHTEEN

SERVING JOYFULLY

Matthew 23:11

"The more lowly your service to others, the greater you are. To be the greatest, be a servant."

My youngest daughter is one of the most naturally selfless people I know. She is patient, flexible with changes, and considerate of other people's feelings. She accepts people just as they are, expects very little from them, and is the first to step up and help. I know she doesn't get these amazing qualities from me. It's definitely a God thing.

James 1:17 says God is the giver of every good and perfect gift. Although each one of us is unique and uniquely gifted by God (Rom. 12:6–8), what is common to us all is that we are called to follow Jesus's example. This means we are called to serve. In His strength and for His glory (1 Pet. 4:10–11).

Many of us think about serving in terms of working in our church or out in the community, performing self-sacrificial and honorable works like feeding the poor, collecting blankets for the homeless, or perhaps setting up for communion service. But what about at home or work? We don't always consider those places to be places of "service." Instead, we often view them as roles we have been given with duties we must perform. Unfortunately, this mindset not only diminishes our peace but compromises the works themselves so that we and those we serve lose out on God's richest blessings.

Colossians 3:23–24 says, *"Work hard and cheerfully at all you do, just as though you were working for the Lord and not merely for your masters, remembering that it is the Lord Christ who is going to pay you, giving you your full portion of all he owns. He is the one you are really working for."*

Whether it's at home, at church, in the community, or at our workplace, serving is not so much about what we do but how we do it. Do we do it willingly, knowing that God has placed us right where we are for a reason and a season? Or do we do it grudgingly, grumbling and mumbling about having to do that second load of dishes or run yet another report for that demanding boss? I have found that when I do the former, I enjoy God's peace and reap the blessings of serving, regardless of what I'm doing. But when I give in to the latter, I struggle to find peace and become sour. God's way is the better way. It is the way of peace.

There were times in my life when I felt like I wasn't that useful for the Lord. As a stay-at-home mom raising two young girls, I thought I wasn't doing enough and was easily intimidated by the women who cared for their family *and* worked outside the home. They seemed to be able to juggle everything much better than I could. Or when I suffered from burnout and chose to scale back on my outside obligations, I entertained the notion that because I wasn't out serving in the community or at church serving, I wasn't doing anything worthwhile. I struggled because I had been approaching service from a perspective of works and not grace.

God's Word says that we are saved by faith and not by works, so that no one can boast (Eph. 2:8). I'm learning that God wants me to serve Him out of love and not fear. The Bible makes it clear: there is nothing you or I could ever do, or not do, that would change God's love for us, because God *is* love. His undeserved favor is the result of who He is, not what we've done. It's a truth that is quite liberating, really. Once I started settling into His unconditional love more, I became less concerned with what I did and more with how I did it.

You don't have to sit on the church board or work at the homeless shelter to be useful for God. While those things are important, and may be a part of your life at some point, serving in more informal ways but with a joyful heart is something we all can do, if we choose the right mindset.

Serving selflessly and cheerfully may not come as naturally to you or me as it does for my daughter, but that shouldn't stop us from serving. We must endeavor to make it a natural part of our daily lives, because God has called us to it. Wherever we are and whatever we do, let's remember that, ultimately, we are serving the Lord.

MY DAILY BREATH

1. **Listen to "Do Something" by Matthew West.**

2. **Memorize 1 Peter 4:10,** *"God has given each of you some special abilities; be sure to use them to help each other, passing on to others God's many kinds of blessings."*

3. **We can serve anywhere, anytime. It doesn't have to be within the confines of the church walls or within the walls of a school or community center. Raising children is a good work. Working gladly at our jobs is a good work. Giving generously with a cheerful heart is a good work. It's about a mindset that is eager to serve God, listening for His voice, ready to step out in obedience— to wherever or whomever He calls us. How might you need to change your perspective on serving?**

FINANCIAL WELLNESS

Tools for Security

"If your profits are in heaven, your heart will be there too."
Matthew 6:21

DAY NINETEEN

HEALTHY BOUNDARIES

Proverbs 21:20

The wise man saves for the future, but the foolish man spends whatever he gets.

Money continues to be the most frequently cited cause of stress for Americans today.[1] Since there is a known connection between chronic stress and disease, it's important to address this little animal before it turns into a beast. Because, if left unchecked, it could rip the peace of God right out of our hands and destroy our health.

I have found that when I'm stressing about money, my ability to trust God in all areas of my life is difficult, if not impossible, and my outlook on just about everything changes. It's as if I start clinging too tightly to everything, afraid I will suffer loss of all kinds. For me, financial stress paints a mindset of lack that colors everything I see around me.

I think one of the reasons why finances rank so high on the stress meter is because it is so foundational to the rest of our lives. It's what keeps food on the table, a roof over our heads, and clothes on our bodies. It also affords us the luxuries that we feel we can't live without. Or, at least, don't want to try to live without. And, in theory, it could keep us from realizing our fullest potential because if we lack the necessities of life, then chances are good we won't have the motivation and resources to invest in higher-level needs such as social intimacy and the opportunity to discover our gifts and talents and use them for the greater good and for God's glory.

However, for most of us, I don't believe the root of our financial stress is about the amount of money we make at all. If that were so, people in other parts of the world living on much less wouldn't still be about as happy as most Americans. The real issue is our approach to money. It's about failing to set healthy boundaries.

As Christians, we can be loving and kind and still set boundaries. Jesus did. He prioritized time with God. He said no to the cynics and those who had inappropriate agendas for him (Luke 23:8–9, Matt. 16:23). He told his disciples to shake the dust off their feet when someone didn't welcome them rather than wringing their hands in worry or trying to persuade them (Matt. 10:14).

Boundaries are simple guidelines and limits we put in place to create and improve our sense of security. As in all other aspects of our lives, we must have them in our finances to remain stable and enjoy the peace of God. The first step is creating a budget.

Yes, the dreaded "B word." I said it. And, I'll admit, I've never been great about creating one or sticking to one. It's a work in progress for me, but I do know that when I "deprive" myself of things that I don't need, I feel more at peace and more satisfied with my life. It's a paradox, really. The more we have, the more we want, and the more we deny ourselves, the more we will delight in the things that really matter.

It goes along with what Jesus said in Mark 8:34–38 when he commanded us to deny ourselves and take up our cross daily, which I interpret to mean treasuring Jesus more than anything in life, including our money, comforts, and possessions.

Now don't get me wrong, I'm not saying that we can't have nice things or that money is evil. Money is necessary, and we can certainly use it to bless others. The key is finding a balanced approach that begins with recognizing that God is our Source and the only One who provides for our needs.

Philippians 4:19 says, *"And it is he who will supply all your needs from his riches in glory because of what Christ Jesus has done for us."*

That's why I believe setting up a budget should start with prayer. If you are like me, it can be too easy to go to one extreme or the other with finances: either living lavishly, with an eat, drink, and be merry mentality, or holding too tightly to our resources for fear of loss, being stingy with what we have.

If you are struggling with your finances today, remember that God is a God of grace, and He is the giver of every good and perfect gift, including the wisdom you need to manage your finances well. And if you have made some colossal mistakes with your finances, remember that it's never too late with God. Be honest with yourself, pray for strength, and set up that budget, choosing to trust that God will give you the grace to stick to it. And should you find yourself struggling to make ends meet, pray in faith that God will provide. He is able and He is faithful.

"Look at the birds! They don't worry about what to eat—they don't need to sow or reap or store up food—for your heavenly Father feeds them. And you are far more valuable to him than they are" (Matt. 6:26).

MY DAILY BREATH

1. **Listen to "Your Grace Finds Me" by Matt Redman.**

2. **Meditate on 1 Timothy 6:10,** *"For the love of money is the first step towards all kinds of sins. Some people have even turned away from God because of their love for it, and as a result have pierced themselves with many sorrows."*

3. **What boundaries do you need to set up to be healthier in your finances? Is it time to set up a budget? If so, start with prayer and ask for God's grace to move past the instant gratification, buy now, pay later mentality that is so prevalent in our culture.**

DAY TWENTY

DIVINE CONTENTMENT

Ecclesiastes 5:10

He who loves money shall never have enough. The foolishness of thinking that wealth brings happiness!

I read a startling statistic. American families who earn at least 10,000 dollars per year are wealthier than 84 percent of the world. Increase that income to at least 50,000 dollars and they make more than 99 percent of the world.[1]

Realistically, most of us in America will never have to suffer extreme need. The United States is the thirteenth richest country in the world,[2] yet studies show that we are not necessarily any happier than other, less affluent, nations.[3]

Why is that?

I think Ecclesiastes 5:10 encapsulates it well when it describes a person with a heart that is bent toward the love of money and possessions. The writer refers to this person's insatiable pursuit of "more" as meaningless. It's meaningless because things are temporary and were never designed to satisfy us. Only God can truly satisfy the longings of our hearts, and trying to find our satisfaction in anything else will surely breed discontent and chip away at the peace He offers to us freely. Really, satisfaction is not about our circumstances but about the condition of our heart. What do we love and what do we pursue with all our heart?

One of the verses I've been standing on this past year is Hebrews 13:5–6:

"Stay away from the love of money; be satisfied with what you have. For God has said, 'I will never, never fail you nor forsake you.' That is why we can say without any doubt or fear, 'The Lord is my Helper, and I am not afraid of anything that mere man can do to me.'"

I stand on this verse, cling to it, and recite it every day, because contentment does not come easy for me. I am always looking to try new things, and I tend to get bored easily. I also have a nasty habit of comparing myself with others, which I have found to be one of the surest ways to compromise my contentment, and one of the quickest ways to dive deeper in debt, as I strive to fill my life with possessions I'm certain will satisfy.

Let's face it; we are a society obsessed with "stuff." Some call it keeping up with the Joneses. I call it a peace thief. We look at our neighbors, coworkers, and friends, and we covet them. We want what they have because they seem to have so much more than we do. And, if you're like me, you question why that is. Sometimes you may even feel like you *deserve* to have more (and thereby justify your purchases), especially if you give your money to the church. At least, that's if you're like me.

I have struggled with this mindset for some time, and I still do at times, which is why I continue to stand on, cling to, and recite Hebrews 13:5–6. Daily. It's a reminder to keep my priorities straight.

"So don't worry at all about having enough food and clothing. Why be like the heathen? For they take pride in all these things and are deeply concerned about them. But your heavenly Father already knows perfectly well that you need them, and he will give them to you if you give him first place in your life and live as he wants you to" (Matt. 6:31-33).

Jesus tells us not to be anxious about the temporary things of life: about what we will drink, eat, or wear. He said God knows our needs and that if we seek His kingdom first then our needs will be met. Paul the apostle understood this, which allowed him to be content in any situation. Despite being beaten, stoned, shipwrecked, and impoverished, Paul kept his priorities straight, and it resulted in a deep-seated peace that nothing in the world could uproot.

Being content is a choice. And it's not necessarily about being completely satisfied where you are right now, either. It's about trusting *the* Source of all you have, knowing that His timing and His provision is enough.

I want to remind you that God has a plan for your life, and it goes much deeper than your income or the things you own. He wants to prepare you for eternity—with Him—and if you will take your eyes off the temporary things of this life and keep them on Him, you will enjoy the peace He promises, and you will find greater contentment. Whatever your circumstance and whatever the size of your bank account.

MY DAILY BREATH

1. Listen to "You Are My All in All" by Nichole Nordeman.

2. **Memorize Proverbs 10:22,** *"The Lord's blessing is our greatest wealth. All our work adds nothing to it!"*

3. **Gratitude is the antidote to discontent. People who express gratitude more often are known to be happier and healthier. Whenever you want to complain, think of three things for which you are thankful. If possible, write them down or record them onto your favorite voice app.**

DAY TWENTY-ONE

A CHEERFUL GIVER

Proverbs 3:9–10

Honor the Lord by giving him the first part of all your income, and he will fill your barns with wheat and barley and overflow your wine vats with the finest wines.

In the book *Giving It All Away... and Getting It Back Again: The Way of Living Generously*, David Green, founder of Hobby Lobby, the world's largest privately-owned arts-and-crafts retail chain, writes, *"We are put here on this earth to give, to devote ourselves to a radical brand of generosity that changes lives and leaves a legacy."* [1]

In the book, David shares his inspiring success story: how he came from humble beginnings and through hard work, perseverance, and bold faith grew his makeshift manufacturing operation (located in his living room) into an enormously successful company that now employs 32,000 people in more than 700 stores across forty-seven states.

The son of a small-town pastor, David grew up poor. With five siblings living in a two-bedroom house, he often slept on a rollaway in the kitchen. His family regularly received food donations from church folks (often going weeks without meat), wore hand-me-downs for everything except underwear and socks, and never owned a car. Yet, he describes his parents as some of the most generous people he has ever known, donating almost their entirely weekly salaries back to the churches they served. Their cheerful generosity and heavenly perspective inspired him to live a life of service for the Lord. Not as a minister, but as a businessman.

Early on, David chose to follow in his parents' footsteps and give generously, leaving a legacy of what he calls invisible things. Now a billionaire, and ranked seventy-nine on the Forbes list of the 400 richest Americans, Green donates up to 50 percent of his company's total pretax earnings and has given upwards of 500 million dollars over the years to various ministries.[2] Truly, he is the poster boy for the principle found in Luke 6:38:

"For if you give you will get! Your gift will return to you in full and overflowing measure, pressed down, shaken together to make room for more, and running over. Whatever measure you use to give—large or small—will be used to measure what is given back to you."

Although they started small, the Green family has consistently been generous with their financial resources, and they have been blessed generously. Although most of us will never have to make decisions about how to spend such a large amount of money, God does call each of us to be generous with our own resources.

"And I was a constant example to you in helping the poor; for I remembered the words of the Lord Jesus, 'It is more blessed to give than to receive'" (Acts 20:35).

I don't believe we can be completely healthy in our finances until we adopt the principle of giving generously. Because the way we manage our finances is a huge indication of the condition of our heart. To give freely with a cheerful heart as God instructs (2 Cor. 9:7) shows that we have put money in its proper place: in submission to God. To hold too tightly to our finances, however, shows that we are either afraid that God won't provide or else just don't understand where our blessings come from.

I learned this lesson during a very lean time in our finances. Like most people, we were hit hard with the Great Recession of 2008. I had just graduated with my master's degree, was carrying a significant amount of student loan debt, had two young girls at home, no job, and my husband's company downsized, bringing about a cut in pay and hours. There were months when I had no idea how we would make it, and I was tempted not to tithe. Up until this point in our marriage, we had tithed faithfully (something I had learned from my parents), and although we weren't well-off by any means, we always seemed to have enough, so there was never any question about whether to give.

Now, with barely enough to live on and going deeper in debt, we felt like we had nothing to give and were faced with a hard choice. Would we trust God and give our 10 percent first or would we give from the leftovers . . . if there were any? It wasn't an easy decision, but by God's grace we chose to keep giving in faith. We stood on Malachi 3:10:

"Bring all the tithes into the storehouse so that there will be food enough in my Temple; if you do, I will open up the windows of heaven for you and pour out a blessing so great you won't have room enough to take it in!"

This is the one place where God says to test Him, and that we did. It was hard to give what we didn't have. And I admit, I sometimes resented this command, especially when I saw people who didn't tithe doing much better than us. But, like it or not, I knew we had no choice but to give since we desperately needed a financial miracle, and God was the only One who could provide it.

I can honestly say, He never let us down.

Time after time He provided. It never made sense on paper, but we always had just enough. We had been forced to put our faith to the test, and we learned in a very tangible way that God is faithful, indeed. I discovered that a little with the Lord is so much more than a lot without him.

Being healthy in our finances means being balanced in how we spend our money, but it also means being balanced in how we approach money. Do we hold onto it tightly, either out of fear of lack or lack of faith? Do we put our desires for the "good things" in life over our desire to give to others? Do we recognize that all we have is from God's hand?

The way we spend our money is a sure indication of what we value, and being out of balance in this area will surely steal the peace of God in our lives. The struggle to give is real, especially when you don't have much. But I have learned that when I do give, I enjoy a deeper degree of God's abundant peace, regardless of my bank account balance. And no matter how lean times have been, I have always found God to be a faithful provider. I know you will too.

MY DAILY BREATH

1. Listen to "Word of Life" by Jeremy Camp.

2. Memorize John 1:1–2, *"Before anything else existed, there was Christ, with God. He has always been alive and is himself God."*

3. To be a generous person, we need God. We need Him to reveal what is in our hearts. We need to be consumed with His love and His ways. We need to hear His voice so we can be receptive to those times when He calls us to give. It all starts with Him. It starts with clinging daily to the Word of Life, Jesus Christ.

4. Consider this: church members on average give less today than they did during the Great Depression. Just 2.6 percent today compared to 3.2 percent in 1930.[3] You would think with much higher earning levels and all the latest gadgets and conveniences we enjoy, including smartphones and high-speed internet, we would give more than during a time when finances were so tight for most people that they had to ration their food and basic living supplies. This says something about the condition of our hearts. May we be different. May we be better.

5. A tithe is meant to be designated to the church, which means the foundation of our giving should be in support of our home church. But giving generously also means giving to be a blessing in our communities. There are many worthwhile charities in need of your generosity. Do a quick Google search, and you are sure to find a cause you believe in!

Hebrews 13: 20–21 says, "And now may the God of peace, who brought again from the dead our Lord Jesus, equip you with all you need for doing his will. May he who became the great Shepherd of the sheep by an everlasting agreement between God and you, signed with his blood, produce in you through the power of Christ all that is pleasing to him. To him be glory forever and ever. Amen."

BREATH OF LIFE
Personal Journal

BREATH OF LIFE
Personal Journal

BREATH OF LIFE

Personal Journal

BREATH OF LIFE
Personal Journal

BREATH OF LIFE
Personal Journal

BREATH OF LIFE
Personal Journal

BREATH OF LIFE

Personal Journal

BREATH OF LIFE
Personal Journal

BREATH OF LIFE
Personal Journal

BREATH OF LIFE
Personal Journal

BREATH OF LIFE

Personal Journal

BREATH OF LIFE

Personal Journal

BREATH OF LIFE

Personal Journal

BREATH OF LIFE
Personal Journal

BREATH OF LIFE
Personal Journal

BREATH OF LIFE

Personal Journal

BREATH OF LIFE
Personal Journal

BREATH OF LIFE

Personal Journal

BREATH OF LIFE

Personal Journal

BREATH OF LIFE
Personal Journal

SALVATION

The greatest decision we will ever make in life, and the one that will lead us to a healthier and more peaceful way of living, is the decision to follow Jesus. This decision not only secures our eternity but gives us the grace and strength to enjoy a healthy, balanced life in the seven dimensions of wellness. Right here in the present moment.

Can you say without a doubt that you know Jesus? That He is your Lord and Savior? That you are following Him with a burning passion?

If not, consider these truths taken from the Holy Bible:

"For God loved the world so much that he gave his only Son so that anyone who believes in him shall not perish but have eternal life" (John 3:16).

"Anyone who calls upon the name of the Lord will be saved" (Rom. 10:13).

If you are ready to acknowledge Jesus as the holy Son of God and your personal Lord and Savior, then all it takes is a simple prayer of faith:

"God, I need you in my life. Jesus, I believe that you died on the cross for my sins, that you rose from the dead, and that you are the only way to the Father in heaven. Forgive me of my sins and make me whole in you. I invite you to be my Lord and Savior and ask that you would fill the emptiness within me with your Holy Spirit. Help me to trust you, and help me to understand your word and to receive your grace and unconditional love every day. Thank you, Lord! In Jesus's name, I pray, AMEN!

If you prayed that simple prayer with a sincere heart, then you are a redeemed child of God—welcome to the family! I encourage you to get plugged into a Bible-believing church so you can grow in faith and community.

I would personally like to know if you prayed this prayer. Please send me a note online at https://illuminatecommunications.org/contact/

NOTES

Day 1

1. "Christianity and Stress," Relevant Magazine, September 8, 2005, https://relevantmagazine.com/life/relationship/blog/2179-christianity-and-stress.
2. C.S. Lewis, "C.S. Lewis Quotes," Brainy Quote, accessed August 22, 2017, https://www.brainyquote.com/quotes/quotes/c/cslewis151474.html.
3. Joyce Meyer, (@JoyceMeyer), "Are you ready to have unreasonable peace? Watch the video below! #peace #goodword," Tweet, June 12, 2017, https://twitter.com/JoyceMeyer/status/874315570816090117/video/1.

Day 2

1. Bob Hostetler, ("10 'Breath Prayers'", March 17, 2015, Guideposts, https://www.guideposts.org/faith-and-prayer/prayer-stories/pray-effectively/10-breath-prayers.

Day 4

1. William H. White, "Exercise to Keep Fit," Sports Illustrated Vault, January 17, 1955, https://www.si.com/vault/1955/01/17/554033/exercise-to-keep-fit.

Day 5

1. Daniel J. DeNoon, "7 Rules for Eating," WebMD, March 23, 2009, http://www.webmd.com/food-recipes/news/20090323/7-rules-for-eating#1.

Day 7

1. Caroline Leaf, *Switch on Your Brain: The Key to Peak Happiness, Thinking, and Health* (Grand Rapids: Baker Books Division of Baker Publishing Group, 2013).

Day 8

1. *The Daily Walk Bible* (NLT), (Atlanta: Walk through the Bible Ministries, Inc. and Carol Stream, IL: Tyndale House Publishers, Inc., 2007), 656.

Day 9

1. Alexandra Smith, "Eyes That Saw Horrors Now See Only Shadows," *Long Beach Journal,* September 8, 1989, http://www.nytimes.com/1989/09/08/us/long-beach-journal-eyes-that-saw-horrors-now-see-only-shadows.html.

Day 10

1. Ted Dekker, *The Forgotten Way Meditations: The Path of Yeshua for Power and Peace in This Life*, (Outlaw Studios, 2015), 272.

Day 11

1. "The Father Absence Crisis in America", Statistics and Free Resources, National Fatherhood Initiative, accessed August 22, 2017, http://cdn2.hubspot.net/hub/135704/file-396018955-pdf/RyanNFIFatherAbsenceInfoGraphic051614.pdf?t=1502456790780.

Day 13

1. Susan Cain, *Quiet: The Power of Introverts in a World That Can't Stop Talking*, (New York: Broadway Paperbacks, Crown Publishing Group, Random House, Inc., 2012).
2. Emma Seppala, "Connectedness & Health: The Science of Social Connection," The Center for Compassion and Altruism Research and Education, Stanford Medicine, May 8, 2014, http://ccare.stanford.edu/uncategorized/connectedness-health-the-science-of-social-connection-infographic/.

Day 14

1. C.S. Lewis, Quote from *Mere Christianity*, Goodreads, accessed August 22, 2017, https://www.goodreads.com/quotes/6979-i-am-trying-here-to-prevent-anyone-saying-the-really.

Day 16

1. Confucius, "Confucius Quotes," Brainy Quote, accessed August 22, 2017, https://www.brainyquote.com/quotes/quotes/c/confucius134717.html.
2. Brian Robben, "Not Happy At Work: A Disease Affecting 70% Of Americans," Take Your Success, April 12, 2016, http://www.takeyoursuccess.com/not-happy-at-work/.
3. Rick Warren, *The Purpose Driven Life*, (Grand Rapids: Zondervan, 2002), 67.

Day 17

1. Mark Batterson, *The Grave Robber: How Jesus Can Make Your Impossible Possible*, (Grand Rapids: Baker Books Division of Baker Publishing Group, 2014), 179-80.
2. Nik Wallenda, "Nik Wallenda Quotes," Brainy Quotes, accessed August 22, 2017, https://www.brainyquote.com/quotes/quotes/n/nikwallend445834.html.

Day 19

1. "How Financial Stress Can Harm Your Health," Fox News Health, February 4, 2015, http://www.foxnews.com/health/2015/02/04/how-financial-stress-can-harm-your-health.html.

Day 20

1. Elizabeth Hovde, "Income in Perspective: America's Poor are Among the World's Wealthy," *Oregon Live*, August 4, 2012, http://www.oregonlive.com/hovde/index.ssf/2012/08/income_in_perspective_americas.html.
2. Barbara Tasch, "RANKED: The 30 Richest Countries in the World," *Business Insider*, March 6, 2017, http://www.businessinsider.com/the-richest-countries-in-the-world-2017-3/#14-saudi-arabia-gdp-per-capita-54078-44122-17.
3. Mark Goulston, "Why are American's So Unhappy?" *Huffington Post*, November 25, 2011, http://www.huffingtonpost.com/mark-goulston-md/why-are-americans-so-unha_b_1112384.html

Day 21

1. David Green with Bill High, *Giving It All Away . . . and Getting It Back Again: The Way of Living Generously*, (Grand Rapids: Zondervan, Harper Collins Publishers, 2017).
2. Brian Solomon, "Meet David Green, Hobby Lobby's Biblical Billionaire," *Forbes*, October 8, 2012, https://www.forbes.com/sites/briansolomon/2012/09/18/david-green-the-biblical-billionaire-backing-the-evangelical-movement/#75a1d2b65807.
3. Green and High, *Giving It All Away*.

CARING THROUGH SHARING

Perhaps you would like to share this book with friends, family, or colleagues. Because I believe in the power of God's Word, and the benefits of a healthy lifestyle, I have created a "Caring Through Sharing" opportunity.

For each set of seven books that you purchase with the intent to give away, we will provide a 50 percent discount off the regular purchase price.

Contact me directly at https://illuminatecommunications.org/contact/ for details.

HEALTHIER LIVING

Ready to move into greater wellness?

- Enjoy healthy, non-toxic living.
- Experience effective pain and energy management.
- Discover pure, powerful products for every family and lifestyle.

Karen Ferguson is a Young Living independent distributor and a passionate advocate for the benefits of using essential oils. Contact her directly to learn more at https://illuminatecommunications.org/contact/

I hope you found this devotional both an inspirational and practical tool on your journey to greater wellness and peace.

If you have enjoyed this book, will you consider sharing the message with others?

- Write a book review on Amazon or Audible.
- Mention the book in a Facebook post, Pinterest pin, blog post, or upload a picture through Instagram.
- Tweet "I recommend reading #breathoflife by @illuminatecomm1."
- Recommend this book to those in your small group, book club, workplace, or classes.

Made in the USA
Columbia, SC
04 August 2019